GOD + MILITARY SPOUSE

GOD + MILITARY SPOUSE

UNITED OUR FAMILIES WILL STAND

KATHLEEN CLINE

HighWay
A division of Anomalos Publishing House
Crane

HighWay
A division of Anomalos Publishing House, Crane 65633
© 2008 by Kathleen Cline

All rights reserved. Published 2008
Printed in the United States of America
08 1
ISBN-10: 0981764355 (paper)

EAN-13: 9780981764351 (paper)

Cover illustration and design by Steve Warner

A CIP catalog record for this book is available from the Library of
Congress.

To my husband and best friend:

God did not bless me with children, but He certainly gave me a great love.

You set such an example for me with your unending gift of caring for others, and somehow you still have enough love for me. I am always impressed by your support and encouragement. Even with all the ups and downs in our marriage, I would not change one day.

Thank you seems so shallow.

With all my love.

Contents

Preface

I have been married to a Navy man for twenty years. I have seen families bond together and I have seen families fall apart. Marriage to a military person is a commitment that will literally make or break you.

If you are breaking apart, don't stop reading. We have all been there. Get through this breaking point, and, I promise, you will be proud of yourself. Let us just make sure you get through your rough patch with your self-worth still intact. I am not saying you will not bear some mental bumps or bruises; those can be repaired. You just do not want to sell out your beliefs.

Now, the older wives know what I am talking about. The younger and less-seasoned wives are probably thinking, *I would never think about selling out any beliefs.* Well, ladies, never say never. When you have been alone for six months, nine months, a year, even 18 months, you and all your relationships will be pushed to a point you would never have thought possible. Even your blood relatives will test you in ways you never thought possible. Why? Unless you have lived a military life, you really do not understand the stress.

Military wives are not just lovers and mommies. When the spouse is on deployment, wives step up to every job you can list in a relationship, 24/7, with the added stress of "is he coming home alive?"

I'm not trying to sound too callused, but deployment used to just mean a prayer of "help my husband remain faithful God"; now the fear of capture, torture, dismemberment, or death seams to diminish, but not eliminate, the original fear.

Hopefully in the next few chapters, we can approach all the issues that military wives face and give it a biblical solution. During the process, I hope you build a bond with other Christian military wives and find support and strength in Christian relationships. You may not have your blood relatives around you, but God is good about bringing you family in the form of friends.

The best way to fight the devil and all his temptations is to cling to God and accept all the support He sends your way. Do not be proud; we all need help once in a while. Can you think of a better way than with Christian women who are in the same situation or have been in the same situations?

This book is written in simple lessons—simple because the basics are what are important in this world. This leads to a strong, stable foundation. You could have all the advanced mathematical education this world can offer, but if you are unable to calculate 2+2, then your results are flawed. The same could be said for your marriage. It is your attitude that sets the tone. It is your ability to be grateful, no matter what comes your way. It is the simple sins that you have allowed into your life and deem benign that have poisoned your life. It is the little bricks of life that you have laid, not God that has sent you, on a path of a rocky marriage.

God bless you and the words you are about to read. May the Holy Spirit guide your heart to the path you need to follow. Please, Heavenly Father, bless our men and women who are serving you and the country. Give us strength to fight when we need to fight, love when we need to love, and compassion for all.

Introduction

God led me to write this book for military wives. I began to notice that there were books for women, but none specifically for military women.

When the war first broke out, there was ramped support for the military. However, as we are nearing four years, I feel now, more than ever, that we need support and it is not there. I am not talking about supporting the troops by putting a ribbon on your bumper. We need support coming from Christian women who have been there and can witness how God got them through their long deployments.

My hope is that women form small groups, begin to pray as military spouses, and form strong Christian bonds to support each other. We all have special needs. Some couples are on multiple deployments now; others have finished multiple deployments and now are facing a year to eighteen-month tour. Even when our spouses are serving duty at home, they are filling in for the deployed members. Therefore, working hours are strenuous at best.

Divorce is high in the military, and no one is talking about it. Families are being pushed to new territories and society is ignoring it. Society barely understands why any intelligent person would join the military, so why should they be concerned with the families?

God has guided me to share my experiences, along with verses, to help you succeed not only in your career, but the military career of your spouse as well. The two of you are in this together. If you are not fully committed to this venture, there will be one more failed marriage.

As a Christian, you need to take your vows seriously. "For better or for worse" is a powerful statement. I bet no one explained to you how lonely you would be as a military spouse. All the responsibilities of marriage without the fringe benefits are a lot to take on for any person.

Many of you ladies are young and coming from broken families, so you may not see the great loss if your marriage fails as well. It is so easy to walk away from any relationship, but what does it say about your character? It is hard to be a military wife, but with this job comes great pride. I have grown so much in my life, both spiritually and emotionally. The military life will do that to you. The one thing I have learned as an independent military wife is that I do not *need* my husband; I chose to be with him. Unfortunately, I think this thought is the beginning of most divorces.

A young girl gets married and moves away from home. She has never been away from home, and she clings to her husband on this new adventure. Somewhere along the line comes a deployment. The young wife is scared, but through the deployment she discovers that she is strong and surviving just fine. Like many young wives, she forgets that she is married and should not carry on as if she were single. Her husband is deployed and her job, as his spouse, is to hold things down while he is gone. She is not to party every night on his wages. Through her independent discoveries, she decides that she does not need her husband and thus starts the split. Instead of putting the marriage first, the young girl puts her fleshly needs first. That one wrong step can lead to a spiraling effect on her marriage. She went from a couple mentality to a single mentality. This is easy to do in a military marriage, because the wife is left holding down the home quite a bit.

This is where I think Christian support groups are very important. Support groups will help you maintain your focus on your family and your husband, and not on what your flesh is telling you. It hurts to go to bed alone. It hurts not to have someone to touch you.

I have no children, and I remember almost sitting on

my friend during church while my husband was on tour in Iraq. Her husband was gone for a year and mine for six months. Sometimes I would hold her hand during church. This is funny only to me because I am not a touchy feely person. However, God gave me a friend that let me get the personal touch I needed. It was not the same as my husband's touch, but it was sustaining enough to get me through.

If you are determined not to walk away from your marriage and to plough through the bad times, you can do it. I remember an anniversary card that my husband gave me during a pretty rocky time in our marriage. It is a couple on a roller coaster, and when you open the card they are clinging to each other, and the caption says, "Here we go again." I think this is a perfect depiction of what marriage in general is about: the coaster representing the ups and downs in marriage.

Now, let us compound the marriage with long hours during work-ups, and separation during deployments. If you do not figuratively cling to each other you will begin to live separate lives.

Separate lives are a new common phenomenon in the military marriage. We used to see couples separated because the member received unaccompanied orders for a year overseas. Now we see couples, or even families, separating because the spouse does not want to move with the member. The excuses are that the spouse has a great paying job, the kids are in school, or the tour is on a different coast away from extended family. I am talking about the family being separated by miles as a choice.

I remember last Christmas standing at the Command party and talking with another couple on this topic. We could name several couples that we knew who were choosing to take this separation as a life choice. It has become a common practice, and how can this not scare people? I am talking about couples separating for a full three-year tour in different states. Is this the new way that the devil has invented to collapse the Christian military family?

Hopefully, we can try and save one marriage at a time through getting together and taking *to God* all the issues that the military families are facing. By getting together with other Christian women, you can begin to discuss your experiences and take your needs *to God*. We need to build a strong force against the devil, who is slowly and methodically tearing apart our families. Society does not care, so it is time to step up and say enough is enough. What God put together, let no man pull asunder.

Pre-deployment Mood

The wise woman builds her house,
but with her own hands the
foolish one tears hers down.

—Proverbs 14:1, New International Version

Wow, did you think you had that much control in your house? Well, ladies, we do. So, you need to determine how the next few months are going to go. The orders are in and you do not like them.

Now I am going to stop here for a minute. Speaking from experience and actually verbalizing these dumb words myself: "You need to go and tell them you don't like these orders. It is not fair; you deserve better than these orders." Now I am being kind. The last statement is mild and short. Ladies, do you really think your husband can go and tell anybody anything?

You know your rant could last up to an hour and if you are a brooder, your tantrum will droll on for weeks.

How fair are you being to your husband? Turn the tables. If these were your orders and he was carrying on for weeks, how would you feel? Let me take a stab at how you make him feel. Maybe he would feel like he just let you down. Maybe he would feel worthless and that you have no respect for him.

The truth is, most of the time all we are feeling is helplessness. We have no control in our lives. It doesn't even have to do with our husband as much as a lack of control in our own lives.

We have such little control in our duty stations and time there, that for sanity's sake, we control the smallest detail we can possibly predict. So when we do not like the military's choices, to make ourselves feel better, we tear anyone and everyone apart. But seriously, how much better do you feel?

Now, you may not feel this way for every billet you get. You may not have experienced this exact feeling, but I know from being a female that you have tormented your husband concerning a choice he has made in your marriage. My point is, are you tearing your house apart or are you building your house up?

I have learned something through the years about military orders. You can go kicking and screaming or you can just go with a little dignity intact. There is a funny thing about having God in your life. If you are quiet for a while, He will show you that He is in complete control. Shock of all shocks, you might even enjoy yourself. This can apply to any aspect of your life if you would be still long enough and let God have control—not a co-pilot—complete control.

Deployments are a tad different, but there is no reason you and you husband cannot set goals and make plans that the two of you can work toward while he is deployed. You cannot do this if you are tearing your own house down with your attitude.

When you have received the news of his deployment the tendency is to push your husband away, because it will make it less difficult to say good-bye. Where on earth did we get this stupid idea? Let me save you from yourself. It doesn't work. All you will feel when you go to say good-bye is guilt for wasting precious time and the same sadness that was already going to be felt.

An attitude I have begun to work toward in my life is each day when I go to bed, if I can lay my head down and be proud of my behavior that day, it was a good day. Not that everything went well during the day. My day could have been a complete nightmare. That is not what matters. What matters is that I did not tear down my own house. In other words, I maintained a Christian attitude. "In your anger do not sin…" (Eph. 4:26, NIV). Your behavior and reaction to life is your testimony to everyone around you.

I had a friend that was on terminal leave. He was retiring from the Navy and going to start his own business. Sorry to say, the Navy had other ideas. He was pulled off terminal leave and given orders to Kuwait. Thank God just for six months, but six months all the same.

Now when his wife, my best friend, called to tell me the news, there was no ranting involved. There were tears and a complete confidence that God was in control. Tears are normal, ladies. In fact, there is nothing wrong with any of our emotions. God gave them to us for a reason. It is how we project our emotions that get us into trouble. During that deployment, my best friend was able to save even more money, which can now go toward her husband's business.

No one knows how my friend and his wife's reactions toward this change of plans witnesses to others. Only God knows these things. That is why it is important to remember that your behavior and reaction to life are your testimony to everyone around you.

You need to determine right now who is in control of your life. If you really believe it is God, then you need to ask yourself if your reaction reflects that belief.

I am not talking about tears or sadness. I am talking about that destructive behavior that comes out and says evil things—that hateful creature that not even you can stand; the one that spews hate because you are not happy.

You need to take a stand to stop tearing down your house. When you hear the Holy Spirit say stop, you stop, even in mid-sentence. Apologize. Take a breath. This is a process that needs to be learned. If you earnestly seek God toward your attitude, I promise you the Holy Spirit will convict you on the spot. Your job is to listen, stop your action, and correct any damage done at that very moment. It may be very humbling, but you need to make a choice. "The wise woman builds her house, but with her own hands the foolish one tears hers down" (Prov. 14:1, NIV).

I cannot express how proud I am of my husband. God has called him to his field and to serve in the Navy. You, too, should feel this sense of pride. When you receive your next orders, remember there are two of you serving. Your husband has accepted his orders without wavering and so should you. It is okay to be sad, scared and every other emotion that surges through our chaotic bodies. Give them to God. He is in control. God will give you all the comfort and peace you need. And believe me, God sends you support from friends, family and people you may not expect.

Praise God.

1. What were the worst orders you have gotten to date?

_____

_____

Were you proud of your reaction? If not, in the future how can you correct your attitude?

_____

_____

2. Who has control of you, your emotions or God?

_____

Are you proud of your behavior, or has pride blinded you as to how you really look in the heat of the moment?

_____

_____

_____

3. If you have children, would you want them to immolate you in a crisis?

_____

_____

_____

POINT TO PONDER

Why do you verbally draw blood when you are mentally hurt? Do you think it is healthy that you want to hurt the people around you? Why do we verbally shred people apart, especially when we claim to be Christian? Does "sorry" ever take back the pain of verbal abuse?

I Never Thought I Could Feel So Sad!

Rejoice in the Lord always. I will say it again: Rejoice! Let your gentleness be evident to all. The Lord is near. Do not be anxious about anything, but in everything, by prayer and petition, with thanksgiving, present your request to God. And the peace of God, which transcends all understanding, will guard your hearts and your minds in Christ Jesus.

—Philippians 4:4–7, NIV

It is hard to explain the emptiness that you feel when your spouse first deploys. It is like someone cut a hole into your soul. When my husband left for Iraq, I cried so hard I almost vomited. And that is saying something, because I am not a crier.

Soon came the empty feeling with overwhelming sadness. I was so sad that I did not want to cry. It was a weird sensation. It is almost like exhaustion, but it isn't physical, it is completely emotional.

Now, how am I supposed to be thankful to God at this moment in time? Easy. I could take solace in the fact that I knew, without a doubt, that my husband and I were doing exactly what God had planned for us. You see, eight months before the work-up started and then the deployment, I was standing in my husband's boss's office. It was our welcome aboard.

In this office, his 06 was explaining in great detail what his plan was for the office and for my husband. "Don't worry" he said, "your husband is not deploying this year. I need him here while I deploy to Iraq. He will deploy in a year and a half from now when I get back." This made me happy, since my husband and I wanted to try to adopt a child. This would give us enough time to get things started.

Then one evening about a month and half later, my husband offered to do the dishes for me and told me to sit down. Believe it or not, this gesture alone did not alert me to something being up. As my husband washed the dishes, he began to explain the Marine Corps to me. I was completely fascinated, because he was explaining to me how the MEU (Marine Expeditionary Unit) forms. I have never heard of such a thing. In the Navy you have your orders and without an act of God, your command has you for a minimum of two of your three years. In the same tone, he had been talking about the MEU, he said, "The MEU requested me, and I leave for Iraq in the fall. Work-ups begin in a month." Believe it or not, in the same calm voice I was talking in, I said, "I guess it is God's will." I felt it in my soul.

So, it is your first month alone, and I am telling you to rejoice in the Lord. Well, do it, honey. God really does give you a peace that you cannot explain to anyone. You have to experience it for yourself.

I have been in situations that I was not happy about and when I calmed down enough to think, I remembered to thank God. I may not understand why I was going through the situation, but I thanked God for the situation just the same.

You see, we cannot see the future. Oh, we can attempt to plan and maneuver our lives in certain directions, but we have no clue what tomorrow brings. And those "situations" are God's way of preparing us for the future. "Situations" could also divert us from certain harm. Ask the people late for work on 9/11.

Every time you are standing in the unknown, this is when you should especially thank God. You should know in your heart that this is for God's will and for His glory. This is not about you; it is about God. This is why you should be proud of yourself and your husband. The two of you are not just serving your country, you are both serving God and country. Despite what the liberal media and government is trying to feed you, this country was built for God. That is why our country was so successful from the start. God was placed in all aspects of America. One nation under God, and the two of you are sacrificing for God and country.

"But I am afraid he is going to die."

This is a non-verbal taboo thought in the military. You do not go there; you do not speak about it. You can't for your own sanity and your husband's. Positive thoughts are the only thinking allowed.

I remember when the war first started. I was not too worried, because my husband was in a program that made him ineligible to go to Iraq at that time. However, my friend's husband, who was also in a non-deployable billet, was grabbed for the first wave. The first lesson for all of us in war is that there is no such thing as a non-deployable billet.

This was new territory for both my friend and I. We were the Navy, and our husbands went out on big strong ships. However, this time my friend's husband was "boots on the ground" with the Marines.

I remember talking to her on the phone while her husband was up in the high desert waiting to be sent over. The one statement I remember that she shared with me was if he died, how proud she was of him, because he was doing what God meant for him to do. Think about this for a minute, ladies. Some of your husbands have been serving in the military for years, training, just for this call. Some of your husbands are entering the military just for this call. It is a sacrifice that no civilian can understand.

So, while you're anxious about the loss of your husband or your children's father, remember the verse: "Do not be anxious about anything, but in everything, by prayer and petition, with thanksgiving, present your request to God. And the peace of God, which transcends all understanding, will guard your hearts and your minds in Christ Jesus" (Phil. 4:6–7, NIV).

I was so out of my realm when my husband left for Iraq that I started sleepwalking. Thank God it was winter so when my feet hit the cold hardwood floor, it woke me up. It took a month of prayer and complete resolution to God before it stopped.

It is funny when you think about it. What does worrying accomplish? Does it make your husband safe? We are military wives. Woman of action. We are planners, mothers, lovers, fathers, bill payers, sometimes breadwinners, but never women of giving up. So why on earth do we give in to our worries? It is the devil's way of making us weak. We can be concerned about our husband's well being, but to give into worry is giving up all hope.

When we go to God with prayer and petition, we have hope. Even if something happens to our spouses, we have the knowledge that God is near. There is a plan. Take pride in knowing your spouse willingly joined the military knowing what was at stake and still with all that knowledge, he is proud to go to war and serve.

During deployments it is important to have a strong Christian support group. Prayer is the only way to bring some peace into your life. If there is not a group in your area, take the opportunity to start a group. You may not have to lead. Many people just need someone to organize, then others begin to step forward to take other jobs that need to be filled.

Partying, alcohol, shopping and eating will not fill the sad void you are feeling. God can fill that void. There is nothing on earth compared to the peace of God.

1. Write a testimony about your Iraq deployment
   or any other separation you have experienced.
   (Hopefully, you will release some tears through
   this process.) Just thank God.

   _____

   _____

   _____

2. Can you recognize some other emotions caused by
   the deployment?

   _____

   _____

   _____

3. Have you laughed today? Why not?

   _____

   _____

   _____

4. What is your biggest fear? Have you given it to God? If no, then why not?

_____

_____

_____

POINT TO PONDER

"Saying it out loud will make it come true." Are you a god? Are you confusing prophesying with the theory of positive thinking? Are you worshipping a vicious God? Do you believe Philippians 4:4–7?

Then take your troubles to God and stop giving the devil a foothold with your worries.

THREE

What Has God Asked You to Build?

And you, my son Solomon, acknowledge the God of your father, and serve him with whole hearted devotion and with a willing mind, for the Lord searches every heart and understands every motive behind the thoughts. If you seek him, he will be found by you; but if you forsake him, he will reject you forever. Consider now, for the Lord has chosen you to build a temple as a sanctuary. Be strong and do the work.

—I CHRONICLES 28:9–10, NIV

As Christians, we pray for God's will in our lives. This is what we are taught. But do we mean it? For example, your husband is up for orders and you and your spouse start praying for guidance. You look at your selections, pick out what looks best and make a choice. All is well in your household.

Then the detailer calls and there is a change. You are

now going overseas, or worse yet, your husband is being deployed. "No!" you scream. "This is not fair. My husband has gone twice already. Look at him over there. He has not gone at all." Sound familiar? It should. We do it every day with God.

We pray for His will, and when it comes, we cry because the path is too hard. Somehow it does not fit into our schedule. Sadly, we then do something that is so accepted in our Christian walk; we stall by praying. This answer could not be correct, so you go and pray some more. Understand, you are not praying for clarity, you are praying to get God to change His mind. You tell everyone around you that you want God's will, but you are doing everything in your power to get things changed.

Let us look at the phrase "serve him with whole-hearted devotion and with a willing mind." My question to you today is: Do you have a willing mind? Do you do what is right or do you justify your behavior with an excuse?

We sin and then we make statements like, "I did that because they really deserved that" or "they asked for it." My favorite of all favorites is: "God knows me, and this is the way I am." We always have an explanation or an excuse for our sinful behavior. Is your Christianity a verbal walk or a willing-mind walk?

You may also be questioning, what are sinful behaviors? You may think you not only pray for, but also live, a life in God's will. Political correctness is disliked by most, but have you looked to see how much has crept into your Christian walk?

I am going to skip the hot button topics like abortion or homosexuality. Let us just look at the simple ideas that are completely accepted into our daily lives. Adultery, lying, stealing and coveting are just a few completely normal and accepted ways of life. It is common. In our minds, we have allowed ourselves to accept these actions as normal. We have numbed our minds to the point that we are no longer willing to hear what God has to say with the Ten Commandments, and have allowed society to sway our thinking that the Bible is old fashioned.

To serve with a willing mind is to be obedient to God and what His word has to teach us. "For the Lord searches every heart and understands every motive behind the thoughts" (1 Chron. 28:9, NIV).

Here comes the "ouch" factor. You can justify your behavior to any person, and they may buy what you are selling, but you cannot do that with God. The sad thing is, you can justify your sinful behavior so long that you yourself may actually buy into your excuses. Hopefully, you have not hardened your heart so much that you cannot hear the Holy Spirit. If you earnestly go to God and ask Him to confront your sinful nature, He will guide you.

As Christians, we need to take a stand against what society claims is normal. It is not normal for a married person to have an affair. It is not only destructive to the relationship, but also self-destructive.

It is not normal to take office supplies home because you forgot to buy school supplies. "Who will know" is not an alibi. As a Christian, you are to live by God's standard, and what kind of example are you setting for your children? There is no such thing as a white lie. Finally, if you dislike your neighbor because he has something that you don't, there is a problem.

God blesses us all differently. If you cannot be happy with what you have, then how can God bless you? Let me help if you still do not understand.

Happiness as a Christian does not come from possessions. If you are so focused on earthly things, then you are worshipping the wrong god. I am not saying you cannot appreciate nice things, but when an inanimate object brings jealousy and hate into your life, you need to pray for God to refocus your thoughts.

That is where the third phrase comes into play. "If you seek him, he will be found by you but if you forsake him, he will reject you forever" (1 Chron. 28:10, NIV). This phrase is talking about total rejection. If a person rejects God in this life, it will lead to total separation in the afterlife. The only way to prevent being separated from God in the afterlife is to be saved. I think it important to give the salvation plan as often as you are given the opportunity. Never assume because someone is in church that they are saved.

I visited a friend's church one Sunday, and they had a member of twenty-five years walk down the aisle for an altar call. Never let your pride keep you away from God. Is your appearance to others or being worried about gossip really worth eternal damnation? "That if you confess with your mouth, 'Jesus is Lord,' and believe in your heart that God raised him from the dead, you will be saved. For it is with your heart that you believe and are justified, and it is with your mouth that you confess and are saved" (Rom. 10:9–10, NIV). That is the salvation plan.

As a young Christian, I used to think that if I made a conscious choice to sin that God would reject me forever—those all so common "I can do this on my own, I don't need God" moments.

For example, once I was talking with two ladies. We were discussing what had happened in a church meeting. I was expressing a mistake that I had made during the meeting. The conversation was benign, but whom I was talking to was not. The Holy Spirit actually told me to stop. Believe it or not, I stated, "I got it, God. I know what I am doing" in my head. I caused a very big upheaval in the church not by what I'd said, but whom I'd said it to.

They took that information and twisted it to suit their needs. If I had not rejected what the Holy Spirit was trying to say to me, I could have saved a fair amount of heartache. This is true in all our lives. Free will was given to man by God and a wrong choice was man's downfall into sin. Regrettably, we will reject God's will at some point, which will lead to turmoil in our lives, but not a separation from God. If we seek God, he will not leave us.

Verse 10 is the message I would like for you to think about. "Consider now, for the Lord has chosen you to build a temple as a sanctuary. Be strong and do the work."

When you think of God's people that have done great things, who do you think about? Now, stop and think about what is great.

Many of us have chosen to be military housewives and mothers. When we meet other wives that are corporate or professional, we begin to think less of our lives. What contribution does grocery shopping, carpooling, balancing the checkbook and all those mundane jobs that someone has to do, really add to this world? When your child comes home to a safe environment, isn't that sanctuary? When our warriors know they have praying wives who are going to hold down the home while they are at war, isn't that sanctuary?

As women we can dictate the mood of the home, so we can create an atmosphere of sanctuary or hell. We need to stop trying to get acceptance from the world and be proud to serve God in our homes. The pecking order is simple: God then family.

Now, let us take God's will outside the home. You can make or break a stranger's day by a facial expression, verbal exchange or body language. We have more influence in this world than we give ourselves credit for.

"Be strong and do the work" (1 Chron. 28:10, NIV). God is telling us on a daily basis to do His will. Basically, being the best Christian we can be: constantly asking God to guide us. Work is a verb, which requires action. God did not ask us to sit still and pray about it one more time because we do not like His answer.

If you do not like the answer, do as Jesus did in Luke 22:42, New King James Version, where it states, "Father, if it is Your will, take this cup away from Me; nevertheless not My will, but Yours be done."

Now you've got your answer from God. What did God ask you to build?

1. What is your motive when you pray? Whose
   priorities are important when you pray?

   _____

   _____

   _____

2. Name some "normal" behaviors accepted by society
   that God has listed as a sin. What made you accept
   these behaviors?

   _____

   _____

   _____

3. What is a "white lie"?

   _____

   _____

   _____

4. Are wedding vows important?

_____

_____

_____

6. What is your motive behind your thoughts?

_____

_____

_____

POINT TO PONDER

When you go to a social event and someone asks you what you do, how do you answer? How do you feel about your answer? How do you feel about yourself? If you and your family are at peace with God and flourishing, why is society's opinion about your family's choices important?

FOUR

The Purpose of Trials

Consider it pure joy, my brothers, whenever you face trials of many kinds, because you know that the testing of your faith develops perseverance. Perseverance must finish its work so that you may be mature and complete, not lacking anything. If any of you lacks wisdom, he should ask God, who gives generously to all without finding fault, and it will be given to him.

—JAMES 1:2–5, NIV

W hy, when your husband steps out the door for deployment, is it that something major happens? The car breaks down; the washing machine floods. Everyone that has gone through a deployment has a story. I even know two separate families whose family dog was killed during a deployment. You're trying to wrap your mind around why.

Trouble is a daily occurrence in life; some people just seem to get a little bit more than others. Now, be careful here. It is not for you to judge why someone is going through tough times. Go and read about the friends of Job, and when you are done, if you still feel qualified to judge God's motive, good luck.

This is why God is God. He knows exactly what we need in our lives, whether He is forming us with trials to prepare us for the future or straightening us out to draw us closer to Him. Also, God could be working through us to bring someone else to Him. This subject is so complicated, because there're so many possibilities.

If you read on in James, this book goes into detail about God's purpose, God's word, our conduct, our faith—a basic Christian how-to book. Hopefully after you read the book of James, you will understand that God loves you and He is preparing you to complete the task He has set for your life.

"Consider it pure joy" is a funny statement for most and if you had someone say that to you while you were in the midst of a flooded house or broken down car fully loaded with kids and groceries, you might want to scream. You could try and look in the Bible to find how to deal with an appliance or other mechanical failures, but you will not find it.

You will find broad, practical behaviors we are to emulate when we are in trouble. For example, in James 1:19, NIV, it says, "Everyone should be quick to listen, slow to speak and slow to become angry, for man's anger does not bring about the righteous life that God desires."

Let's take the broken-down car example. It has been a long, hot summer day. You have gone to the grocery store because you finally have a moment's peace alone without the kids. On the way back from the store, you pick up your kids at a friend's home. They have been swimming all day and are sugared up from all the junk that the other mother so kindly shoved into them. Some of the kids are tired, some of the kids are hyper and all of them are making some kind of incoherent noise. As you chug along in your six-year-old, paid-off vehicle, the car decides to die. It is a hot day, you have screaming kids, and no spouse at home to call. You think to yourself: *Do I call someone? Who do I call? Can I stand outside and scream without being taken away as crazy?*

This is the most important time to be careful how to react, because you have witnesses. Seriously, your children are watching and learning from your reactions. If your house is flooding and you are alone, it is between you and God. But now your children are watching. You can talk until you are blue in the face, and it will all be mute to your kids if you cannot walk the talk.

I remember once when we went to a store to get three burnt-orange bar stools. That fact alone should date me. Did I mention green stamps? Anyway, my mom locked her keys in the car. We lived in Florida, and it was hot. My dad did not get off work until four, so we sat at the curb of the store on our burnt-orange stools. We had to take turns sitting, because there were only three stools and four people, but I do not remember this experience in a bad light. Now if you were to ask my mom, she may finally express her inner turmoil, but I never saw that. She locked her keys, we sat, Dad came, and we left. No screaming or cursing, probably a lot of correcting of our behavior, but other than that, no bad memories. I even think my dad liked the stools. My point is, how are your kids going to remember this trial? How are the other strangers around you going to remember this incident? Was God the first person you called on, or did you use your cell phone for help?

Now, I know you are going to need your cell phone, but that is not my point. Did you ask God for wisdom? It takes seconds to utter a prayer. "God I need help!"

Now let us talk about being alone when trials come. This, I believe, is a true test of one's character. "No one is here so I can curse and cuss and carry on like a fool and who cares?" Wrong. You need to resolve in your mind right now how you are going to act.

For example, most people are not tempted by stealing. You learned from childhood that stealing is wrong and a crime. You will not benefit from this crime, even if you do not get caught by man. God sees, and you will not prosper from this sin. This is in your head. Therefore, you could sit by your girlfriend's purse all day by yourself and not be tempted to steal.

So why, *why*, do we allow our emotions to get the best of us and we give full throttle to our tongues when things start to go bad? We know that standing in two inches of water using every fowl thing that can flow from our mind to our tongue is displeasing to God, or should I say, a sin!

The really sad thing is, you might even act that way with little ones around your knees. And if anyone went to remind you of the extra pairs of ears, you will justify yourself by saying, "They know better than to use that language." Here are the facts of life. Garbage in: garbage out. You can try and justify your behavior all day long, but your Christian witness to your children now belongs to the devil when you behave like a raging fool.

Your trial that should have been glory to God just gave the devil a stronger foothold on your life. Just because your spouse went on deployment does not mean you are alone in this world. God is one thought away.

God has not blessed my husband and me with assignments near family, but I have to be a witness and say He has always supplied me with a Christian family when I sought Him. I am on my eighth duty station and when

I think back on all the good friends He has blessed me with, it brings tears to my eyes.

Trials are going to happen in your life. It is your choice if you want to make them a learning and growth period or one more behavioral nightmare that the devil uses to haunt you. Once again, if you can put your head on your pillow and be proud of your behavior that day, all and all, it was a good day.

1. What was the first trial during your deployment?

_____

_____

_____

2. Are you proud of yourself and the way that you reacted?

_____

_____

_____

3. How can you learn from this experience?

_____

_____

_____

4. Write a testimony on "how to" or "what not to do."

_____

_____

_____

POINT TO PONDER

From childhood we have beliefs set in our minds that never falter. Why is it difficult to set in our minds the manner we need to conduct ourselves? Why do we give the devil a foothold in our lives with the use of our tongues? What will it take to stop your behavior?

FIVE

In the Midst of the Deployment

Above all else, guard your heart, for it is the well-spring of life. Put away perversity from your mouth; keep corrupt talk far from your lips. Let your eyes look straight ahead, fix your gaze directly before you. Make level paths for your feet and take only ways that are firm. Do not swerve to the right or the left; keep your foot from evil.

—Proverbs 4:23–27, NIV

It is when things are going well in our lives that I think we get into the worst trouble. We are chugging along with deployment, no major crisis, and we start to slowly veer away from God. We begin to take small steps in our choices that begin us on a path away from God.

If life were blatant right or wrong turns, choices would be so much easier, but they are not. It is the subtle changes we make that allow the devil to get a foothold on our lives and before we know it, we are tangled in a big, fat mess.

Or worse, we have walked directly away from God, and we never noticed. First, we stop reading the Word, then the prayers begin to taper off and the next thing we know, we are making all the decisions on our own.

I think this behavior begins once we are comfortable and content with the way things are in our lives. Our focus has changed from completing God's task to completing our own task. But why does it have to be one or the other?

It is simple. We have not completely invited God into our lives. Like many relationships, we keep God one arm's length away from getting too close. We call it wiggle room and so does the devil. You see, our thoughts should be completely linked with God's. This is why it is very important to have a strong church family and Christian women in your lives. They can help keep you accountable.

Many people use the excuse that they do not need to go to church to worship God, but the church family will help you keep that "level path" in your life. It is important to nourish ourselves in Christ. How wonderful is it to be with other Christians and worship God, and to give testimony of God and to be filled with the Holy Spirit? You cannot get that from home, sleeping-in or watching the game. Technology is far too advanced to use sports as an excuse, and you can nap after church.

Ladies, let me make a strong point here. I wrote that

you need Christian *women* in your life. God gives us married folks, *women* as friends, not men. Do not deceive yourself. If you have developed a friendship with a male while your husband is gone, end it now. You will be asking for all sorts of trouble by having this relationship, and it is a relationship. If you have a family male friend that keeps stopping by while your husband is gone, request that he not visit again until your husband returns. Please, do not think that you can handle it.

I have a very dear friend that invited this temptation into her life, and it almost ended her marriage; plus, the toll it will take on your self-esteem is incredible. Having an emotional or physical affair is self-destructive. The self-hate that will come after this betrayal is almost more than anyone can handle.

Heed my words: God gives us female friends, not male. Show respect to your husband and love yourself enough to say no to this temptation. If you notice, I also keep adding Christian in front of friend. This is also important. Once again, you need someone that will pray with you and keep you accountable in your Christian walk. How uplifting is it to call a friend and just talk about all the things that God has done for you? I do this with my mother.

Have you ever had a friend that would beat a dead horse? Say the same thing over and over and complain and whine? It is exhausting. Don't get me wrong—we all need to unload and whine sometimes, but you need that Christian friend that helps you count your blessings.

I had a friend who called me one evening very upset because her husband had gotten scammed in Paris and was out $1,000. My reaction was, "Thank God you had the money so he did not end up in jail or dead." Now, my reaction is something my mom has taught me. Be grateful for what is there. To this day, my friend still reminds me how important those words were to her. It refocused her thought process. She went from wanting to kill her husband to thanking God nothing worse had happened.

Now, I have friends who are not Christians that I socialize with on a fairly regular basis. I thoroughly believe God brings certain people into our lives for a reason and one is to be a Christian influence in their lives. Be careful that you maintain your faith.

For example, I have a dear friend that believes in God but is not saved, yet. I still have hope. Anyway, this friend knew that Tuesday mornings were my Bible study mornings and for some reason that I can only speculate on, she began to plan functions on this morning. She would push hard for me to come to her functions. Thank you, God. He opened my eyes to her and I really held no hard feelings toward this act. I would hold fast and tell her thank you, that I was available any other morning, but not Tuesdays.

This went on for a while and then it stopped. You may think that she was evil, but I don't see it that way.

How many people come in and out of non-Christian lives claiming to be Christians? However, when you look at their walk, they are just the same or worse than the non-Christians. When you claim to be different, people will test you and watch your reactions to see how different your life is compared to theirs.

Believe me, in the midst of a deployment, people will be watching to see what makes you different. Do not be a fake "Christian" with your behavior, because that is a turnoff to me and I am a Christian. Do what the verse above says. "Guard your heart...keep your foot from evil." Let me point out that it is not *if* you fall in your walk, it is *when* you fall in your walk. We are human and we make bad choices that lead to sometimes-public displays. To me, this is when I know that someone has a strong Christian walk. It is how you pick yourself up and refocus life's path that sets an example.

If you saw the Miss Universe contest this year or just the news clips, you saw Miss America fall on the runway. She slipped and then stood straight up again with such grace. She even had control over her facial expressions. She maintained herself with such dignity. She fell, but that is not what everyone talked about the next day. It is what she did afterwards. She did not blame someone for making the floor slippery. She did not nervously laugh and try to play it off as if it were a joke. She maintained her composure and went on with the contest to make the top five. As Christians we need to remember this incident.

When you have committed a sin, do not try and blame someone or something for that sin. If you were wrong, then you need to say, "I was wrong." End of sentence. No, "but if," or "well…" Take ownership of your mistakes. Example: "Wow, I really lost control of my mouth when I said those words. I was wrong and I am sorry."

Now, here is an example of what you most likely will hear from society: "You really made me mad. I am sorry I said those words, but next time you need to watch what you're doing." Sound familiar? There is no ownership in that last statement. Society has told you that statement is an apology, but it is really just a bunch of reasons that you think gives you a right to act a certain way. The verse above gives you prevention methods to keep from sin. They are all actions you need to put into play. God holds you responsible for the sins you commit by not watching your path.

In the midst of your deployment there are numerous temptations, which you are going to be faced with and society deems benign. I am going to list a few, but I think it is real important to get together with other ladies and talk in detail about some of the snares that are out there.

Let's talk about gossiping. I am a Navy gal and we are taught "loose lips sink ships". I have seen this one in action and it can be devastating.

What about going out dancing, especially when alcohol is involved. My question to you is, why do you need to go out drinking and dancing the night before your husband comes home? What benefit comes from this behavior? What harm can come from this behavior?

Then there is letting a male frequently visit when your husband is gone. Ask yourself, why is your husband's friend coming over to check up on you? If you need something fixed in the house, you can call a married male to come over with his wife to repair the object. You may think this is old-fashioned, but if it saves your marriage, you can call it whatever you want.

Once again, I had a dear friend that allowed a "friend" of her husband's to come over and fix things around the house. Then he was coming over to watch TV or play with the kids. Thus, the beginning of an affair. Now you may not end up in an affair, but how is your husband going to feel when you tell him that his "friend" made a move on you. So, prevent all that trouble and tell the "friend" that you will see him when your husband gets back, and that means phone calls, too.

If you see a young girl going down any of these paths, invite her over for a cup of coffee and tell her stories of your deployments. God gives us experience for a reason. Please bless someone else with your knowledge. Get together as group often to talk about how God is moving in your lives. Have a secret sister program that includes prayers and uplifting notes during the deployment. Dedicate yourself to staying on the correct path and protect your marriage and your family.

1. What daily discipline do you practice to stay on God's path?

_____

_____

_____

2. List your Christian friends that keep you accountable.

_____

_____

_____

3. Is it easy for you to apologize when you are wrong? Do your apologies place blame?

_____

_____

_____

4. What temptations have you seen during deployment?

_____

_____

_____

5. How do you feel about dancing and drinking during your deployment?

_____

_____

POINT TO PONDER

How do you feel about a married female having a male friend? Is your argument based on defending your own actions? What is a relationship? What is an affair? An emotional affair?

Is it disrespectful to your spouse to maintain a relationship that has stirred up gossip and an illusion of an affair?

SIX

Knowing God

Consequently, faith comes from hearing the message, and the message is heard through the word of Christ.

—ROMANS 10:17, NIV

My name is Lori Cline. God has blessed me with the insight to write about military life. I write under the name of Kathleen, my middle name, so if you were to meet me in public you would not feel uncomfortable. If you were to ask me what my husband does, I would tell you he is in the Navy. If I could scratch off my blue sticker, I would. When military personnel salute that blue sticker, I smile, wave and say thank you, because it is not me they are saluting, but showing military respect for what that sticker represents. Now you think you know me, but do you really?

I have given you only a small insight of my personal thoughts, but with females, that information alone may constitute a friendship. We are so free with the term "friend" that it can apply to anyone we meet and know two minutes worth of their life. However, what do we need to know to actually know someone?

Maybe we never really know someone, because we place our perception of what that person is in place of who they actually are. Plus, people are famous for putting on faces to please or deceive others around them. We all have those faces. The mommy face, wife face, corporate face, athlete face, social face and the Christian face. While you sit there in denial, let me give you some examples.

Listen to a mom talk politely on the phone then slip her hand over the receiver to give her children that "if you don't stop" look that moms are famous for, and then continue on politely with her conversation.

Has your military husband come home and barked an order at you just like he is still at work? You and your husband are in the car arguing all the way to the party, then both of you get out of the car, slap smiles on your faces, and move through the party as if nothing ever happened. You spit and spew all the way to church, then act as if angels floated you there on a cloud.

We all have those walls of deceit we place up to not let anyone know what is actually going on. The Brits have a sitcom called "Keeping up Appearances" and that is what everyone does to allude to a better life. Maybe our fear is that if we actually let someone in and they get to know us, they may leave, and sadly, this may happen. Most people are so self-centered and have enough problems of their own that they are not willing to take on someone else's problems. Friendships have now become disposable, especially since the building blocks of most friendships consist of a fluffy 10–15 minute conversation maybe once a week.

My mother and I were watching the news the other day and we were trying to figure out why someone was choosing to live a certain way. My mother answered and said, "They must not know God," meaning they probably were not saved. The Holy Spirit got me thinking on this line. Is it really about being saved, as much as they are saved, but do not "know" God?

It is that personal relationship you need with someone to really get to know their likes and dislikes. How many people do you know that proclaim to be "Christian" but do not live a "Christian" life? Most people would judge and say that they were not really saved. I question if they are saved but have not developed a relationship with God.

Have you ever made the statement, "I am her friend, but she is not mine"? With this, you mean that you have shown friendship by letting her in emotionally and have done some service for her, but she never reciprocated.

I believe this is how some people see their Christianity. They think because they go to church and sit in a pew, sing and let out a few acclamations, that God owes them. There is no relationship with God. You may ask, "How can I get to know God?" Easy—read the Bible. This is the only way you can *know* God.

You and your husband can go out and have coffee and talk. When he is deployed, this relationship is now based on emails and letters. It is the same with God. The Bible is God's word. By reading the Bible, you begin to know what God expects from you.

The New Testament gives you Jesus's life on earth; the perfect example of Christian life. Why is it a perfect example? Because every temptation you feel, every pain you feel, all the emptiness or loneliness you feel, Jesus went through on earth (Heb. 4:15–16). He lived to set the example. The last few hours of Jesus's life speaks volumes of the love that God has for you.

Could you sacrifice your only son for sinners? There is a pedophile on death row. Could you give your son to take the pedophile's place? God did!

Jesus, the Lamb of God, was tortured and died to take on the world's sin so the world could have a chance at salvation. If you read the Bible, you will know this.

It makes me smile when you hear ignorant people say, "Well, if they were really saved, they would not have done that." Read the Bible. God's chosen people were the most dysfunctional people. Why? Well, because they were human. But that is what is so wonderful to me. They sinned, but that is not the end of the story. God picked them back up again, dusted them off, and sent them on their way.

I am making light of this to try and make a point. You are going to fail God at some point. Your goal is to never stop trying. If you repent, God is always willing to forgive. "All the prophets testify about him that everyone who believes in him receives forgiveness of sins though his name" (Acts 10:43, NIV).

Unfortunately, we have to live through the consequence of our actions. God does not take those away, but he will never leave you. "The steps of a *good* man are ordered by the Lord, and He delights in his way. Though he fall, he shall not be utterly cast down; for the Lord upholds *him with* His hand" (Prov. 37:23–24, NKJV).

Now you may be thinking, *Where do I start?* I always tell new studiers to start in the New Testament. Get a study Bible to help with any confusing spots. Be careful with reading only Christian self-help books. I got caught in that myself. There are some wonderful books out there, but you still need to know and read God's word.

Set a goal for yourself. "In six months I will read the New Testament." Many Bibles now have a reading schedule already figured out for you in the Introduction. Before you start, make sure to ask God to help you focus and to give you understanding. Your goal is not to get through as fast as you can, but to get to know God. Your nose is in the Bible to build a relationship. Ask God to give you the same passion to read the Bible as you have for the letters you receive from your husband. You know that feeling you get when your friend calls and you drop everything to get to the phone. Pray for that feeling. If you want to build a relationship, you need to put some time into it.

I worked with a woman for three years. I'd wave when I saw her and ask, "How are you doing?" when I passed. I never knew her name. What kind of relationship do you want?

Pick the Bible up and get to know God.

1. What is the difference between a friend and an acquaintance?

    _____

    _____

    _____

2. What are your qualifications for a friendship?

    _____

    _____

    _____

3. Why did God create man?

    _____

    _____

    _____

4. What are some of God's names?

_____

_____

_____

5. Can you explain the Trinity?

_____

_____

_____

POINT TO PONDER

Being a member of a family, you know the happy and sad times in your family history. So if you cannot explain the small details about God, are you an active Christian family member? How do you plan to really get to know God?

SEVEN

Process of Faith

GENESIS 22:1–14

Often I am afraid of writing on a subject due to the fear of someone taking my words and twisting them to excuse their behavior or suit their lifestyle. This is that very subject. I have prayed that my words are used for the purpose they are intended, and not to excuse the slothful or disobedient Christian.

The story of Abraham has always been a sense of inspiration to me. When I hear the story, I can visualize the process Abraham took. God gave Abraham an order. Abraham packed his supplies, traveled three days, gave instructions to his servants, loaded up his son and supplies, and stepped forward to complete his ordered mission from God. It was a process of time.

As a little girl I heard the story, and in my mind when God instructed Abraham, he went that moment to sacrifice his son. But it was not that way. There were days in which Abraham had to maintain his faith, days he traveled burdened with the task. Could you imagine what was going through his head? The strength and courage it took not to bolt? What would you have been thinking while you walked that three-day path?

This is what that story means to me. It is not the end result that is important here; it is that Abraham was willing to complete the task that God had asked him to do. Do you understand what I am saying? It is the process; that is the story. When God called, Abraham said, "Here I am."

To me, the story should not be called "the offering of Isaac," but "the process of faith." Isaac was never sacrificed. If you were to look at the story, Abraham did not complete the task. Why? The task was not the mission; the mission was the process. I need you to understand this so it can be applied to your life.

When we are faithful to God, many times we are sent on missions that have no end. The mission was the task. If we were to look for a tangible fruit from the mission, we would not be able to find one, because we are looking from a human perspective.

We are unable to understand the Holy God mission. Oh, we can speculate, which many of us are good at doing, but be careful here. At no time should we speak for God. It is hard enough for Christians to fight against the world and the devil without you adding fuel to the fire. Prayer, I cannot stress enough, should be implemented before you open your mouth for an important opinion. Unfortunately, we allow ourselves to spew our opinions as gospel. It is really upsetting to me when the opinion is from someone of statute. Make sure, if it is your opinion, to state that up front. Please, also add to your opinion that you would be happy to pray about it.

Do you want to be responsible for derailing a plan that God has placed His hand on? Believe me, God's will, *will* be done. However, there is no reason for you to be knocking the players down with your opinion, especially "in the name of God."

Once, I listened to a testimony from a preacher who shared about her calling from God. When God gave her the mission for her life, she began to tell everyone around her. The result of this excited blab: people turned on her and made fun of her. Why? God did not tell her to go blab her life mission; that sensation to brag came from her flesh.

My point is this: we could save ourselves tons of grief if we would just perform the mission and give testimony after the mission is complete.

Did you hear Abraham say, "Pray for me. I am about to go up and sacrifice my son on God's orders?" I am not saying that you should not have a prayer warrior that is your confidant. I am questioning how big is your circle? If you are placing a request in the church-wide prayer chain, you might pray to see if this is what you should do.

The knowledge that I was writing this book was shared by my husband and my friend. Not even my mother knew and I talked to her every day. I wanted to tell my mother several times but when I prayed about telling her, the desire was taken from me. God is good in this manner. Desires of the flesh can be taken away by God.

Now you are asking, "What is the mission?" I cannot answer that for you. Only God can answer concerning your life. I can help you recognize them. Yes, you heard me, *them*. Very few of us are like the preacher whose life work is the mission. For most of us, our lives *are* the mission.

As we move in and out of people's lives, we are serving God. That is why it is so important to be in tune with God and have devotions every day with God so we can hear what we are to accomplish. God gives us a small request. With each request accomplished comes experience that prepares us for the next step.

Let me give you an example. I have terrible stage fright. I have taken small steps of faith to help in this area, but the fear is still there. When I was living in Seattle, God gave me a dream. I was standing on a stage talking to thousands of people. I woke with a start. My first thought was, "You have got to be kidding me!" Sadly, I did what I've told you not to do and I talked with people about it. With a few exceptions, this blab had very bad results.

What did I do about this dream? The hardest part of trying to complete God's plan for us is figuring out where to start. My husband and I talked, and if God was calling me to the seminary, we decided that is where I should go. My husband had just enough time left on his tour in Seattle for me to go to a seminary school. When I applied to the seminary, the only thing that held me back was my high school diploma. I could not understand why I needed the diploma since I had a college diploma, but I still did everything I could to get a copy of my high school diploma with no avail. The time had passed for admission. Now I understand it was not the school that was the call; it was the call to service. My husband and I were the ones that said seminary, but God just said service.

God has been so good to guide me in the direction of my service. My heart has always been to serve military spouses. God has not only given me vast experiences in my life, but the desire and ability to serve. Some may look at my life and say, "Well, you only tried once to go to the seminary." However, that was not the mission. The mission was for me to step forward and to say, "Here I am." I did that with the attempt to go to school. God then pointed me in the right direction.

I can say the same for my husband and my attempts toward a family. Since we move every two to three years, we have had trouble adopting. Since 9/11, my husband and I fall into a loophole that only the military fall into, since we move too early to establish state requirements. Neither my husband nor I have felt God has told us to give up on a family. Believe me, plenty of people have, but not God. Faith is not about the end result. I have faith that I am to walk this path toward a family whether or not a child is the end result. My faith is based on the fact that I am doing what God asked of me, if for nothing else but to be a witness of His greatness.

While you are trying to figure out your directions, God is faithful in guiding you. Do not get discouraged and say, "That was a bust."

Remember Abraham? The story is about him preparing for the trip, walking three days, then taking his son as a sacrifice to the alter. End of story. The end result does not matter. God took care of the end. Your story needs to be the same. If you are giving the smallest of missions by God, your reply should be, "Here I am." God takes care of the end of the story.

You have to step forward. You have to be faithful and unwavering. What does your three-day walk look like?

1. Have you ever started something you thought was
   God's will that was blocked from all sides? Did you
   just give up or evaluate the situation? If you gave up,
   reevaluate what you thought you heard from God.
   If you have already evaluated the situation, write
   a testimony of the outcome. Ask the Holy Spirit to
   lead you in the writing of the testimony. (Be patient!
   This process may take days, depending on your
   willingness to hear God.)

_____

_____

_____

2. Have family or friends derailed you from your
   mission? Did you ask for advice or was it
   unsolicited? Have you ever given unsolicited advice?
   What was your motive?

_____

_____

_____

3. How does God talk to you?

_____

_____

_____

4. What can you do to hear God more clearly?

_____

_____

_____

POINT TO PONDER

Why do we go to humans for approval when we get a mission from God? Is it our flesh that needs praise? Is it the devil trying to stop the mission?

EIGHT

Thank the Lord for the Small Things

The Lord bless you and keep you; The Lord make His face shine upon you, and be gracious to you: The Lord lift up His countenance upon you, and give you peace.

—Numbers 6:24–26, NKJV

Have you ever wondered why when something good happens in your life most people give "luck" the credit? Are we embarrassed to publicly thank God for things in our lives? Are we worried that people may see us as silly for thanking God for trivial things? Be careful here. I am not talking about empty words to impress the people around you. I am talking about a mind-set and realization that the Lord is blessing and keeping you, even in the small things—that luck is not on your side, but God is on your side.

In this chapter, I want you to think about the daily coincidences that happen. That moment when something happens and you say to yourself, "Wow, that worked out perfectly." Was that the end of your thought or did your mind shift to God? Did you stop and thank God?

Now, I could easily spend this chapter on reminding you to be thankful in all things, but I feel it is important that if you do not grasp the concept of thanking God when things are suddenly coming together for you, then how can you even begin to understand that "thanks" needs to also come when things are unraveling?

You need to learn to be happy in the small things. Maybe you do not see anything in your life that you should give credit to God for. Maybe you really just see things as good fortune.

One morning around ten, I decided to call my friend at work to tell her I would go to dinner with her Friday night. Now, the funny thing about this was that I would see my friend that afternoon, because we exercised together. It could have waited, but God had me call her because she was at a crossroad. She was sitting at her computer praying about an email. God heard her and sent me to help pray with her concerning this dilemma. Some would say this is a coincidence, but my friend and I know better.

God is in that friend that suddenly shows up or calls when you are in need. God is in that check or bonus that shows up just when the unexpected bill does. God is in that stranger that shows up to help when you are stranded. God is in that little voice that quietly tells you which way to turn to keep you from harm's way.

My mom lives alone in Florida. I often drive the I-95 and I-10 to go and check on her. The drive takes a full day and can be a little nerve-racking. I always pray that God will guide me and that I listen to what He says to do. That last statement is the key. I can be a stubborn woman and can often think I know best, especially in the heat of the moment.

This particular day, I was driving through a major construction area. You know, where the large drums are blocking the stall lanes, the road is graded and rough, and the lanes are shifting with old and new markings on the road. I was in the slow lane and was very eager to spot an opening to move into the left lane. And there it was, a nice gap between two semi-trucks. But the Holy Spirit told me to just wait. Now, the stubborn side of me would have said, "Why? That is a good spot, so let's go." Thank you, God; I listened. The first truck went by, and I waited. The second truck went by, and I moved behind him. Then the first truck struck one of the orange drums and threw it straight into the path of the second truck. Being a large vehicle, it bounced off the front of the engine and went straight under his truck, and the truck began to drag the drum. I drive a small Pontiac Vibe. I cannot say that the outcome of a construction drum being tossed in front of me would have been the same. I can only speculate that I most likely would have lost a windshield, along with a two-ton truck less than two car-lengths back, trying not to collide with me. Every time I think of the possibilities that day, I praise God. It still brings tears to my eyes, even today.

Now, a non-believer hearing this story could contribute my waiting to woman's intuition, good fortune, or maybe even a premonition. This is how the non-believer and maybe some Christians think. They believe we are all walking around in some great big game of chance. Some are lucky and others are not.

I find it sad that people do not experience the "peace" that God can give you when times are good and especially when times are bad. I relish in the thought that my all-knowing God is watching and protecting me.

I could not piece my puzzle of a life together as my creator intended. Yes, I will still have a life and yes, it may be by man's standards a good life, but I could have had a masterpiece. By slowly learning to appreciate the small, I begin to build a relationship with God. Then things begin to grow and my relationship begins to grow and before you know it, I am living my life with God, for His glory.

When God looks at my life, I want Him to be pleased. I want Him to see someone who appreciates the small things in life, a person who knows that all things come from Him. When you begin to appreciate and view life from a thankful attitude, the pleasures of society are no longer your main focus.

You will look at that coveted item that you have longed for and realize that the object will not bring you happiness. The small thing called your family relationship is really what is important. God has already given you what will make you happy, you just haven't noticed or appreciated them yet. From society's point of view, if you're lucky, then maybe you will notice. From my point of view, I have faith that a thankful heart will open the world to you.

1. How has the Lord blessed you today?

_____

_____

_____

2. Name the biggest thing God has blessed you with to
   this date?

_____

_____

_____

3. Name the smallest?

_____

_____

_____

4. To you, what does a blessing look like?

_____

_____

_____

5. Name a time when you were in trouble that God brought you peace?

_____

_____

_____

6. Write a thank you note to God.

_____

_____

_____

7. Have your family join in at dinner. Have everyone list something good that happened in their day.

_____

_____

_____

POINT TO PONDER

When you say "thank God" do you mean it, or is it a phrase said like "oh God"? Have you ever considered that you may be taking the Lord's name in vain? Get a dictionary and look up the meaning of the slang you use, for example: gosh, golly. Do you still think that your choice of slang is better?

NINE

What Do You Want to Be When You Grow Up?

*For I know the plans I have for you," declares
the Lord, "plans to prosper you and not to harm
you, plans to give you hope and a future.*

—JEREMIAH 29:11, NIV

No matter what age I am, I hope I always have dreams. The older I get, my dreams tend to get smaller or maybe more realistic. You know when you were younger how grand your dreams were? Maybe you are still young enough to have those dreams of grandeur.

My husband was thirty-one when he went to medical school, and he was not the oldest. The oldest was a fifty-four-year-old lady. So, I guess dreams really are not limited by age. That thought makes me happy, because like most wives and mothers, we have to backdoor our dreams to help a family member reach his or hers. We selflessly put our loved ones first to help them complete their dreams, which at the time was most likely God's purpose for your life. But now it is time for you to step forward and complete the dream that God has implanted in you.

Whether it is fear or just comfort, it is difficult to start something new, especially if you are what some may call "long in the tooth." Does God have something that He has been nudging you to do?

I obviously have started something new, and I have to say the biggest challenge for me is the devil. He has whispered lies, telling me that I will fail, that God does not want me to do this, and that people will laugh and make fun of me. Oh, there are daily barrages of lies that flow in with self-doubt followed by self-hate. I often remind myself that the devil is very good at his craft, but God is God. God is so patient and loving. When I call to Him, God is good about removing the "self" from my head.

See, this is where I fail myself. I am not writing because I am this god with great insight; I am writing out of obedience to God. But I get so focused on "I," that I forget my purpose.

Like many faithful followers, we get so focused on ourselves and the task at hand that we forget why we are doing the task in the first place. This is why so many churches have power struggles and splits, because the followers forget to follow God. They grabbed the task that was assigned by God, then ran and forgot Who sent them there in the first place. The "self" becomes the focus. So the devil may whisper the lies, but if we were not so focused on the "self," what damage could those lies cause? I am going to revise my biggest challenge to being self-involved.

God gives all people a talent. Some talents are more apparent than others. Churches are very good about giving classes on finding your gifts. I, myself, have taught a class concerning this subject. But as Christians, what do you do with this information? Hopefully, you would start applying those talents or skills toward helping the church body.

Have you ever thought that God is preparing you for more? My natural talent is organization. I do not need to work at organizing; it comes as naturally as breathing for me. I can look at a situation, pile of work, room or a task, and can easily see a solution for organizing. Naturally, I then organized whatever was needed in church, whether it was cleaning closets or to help design and execute VBS. I would put my gift to use. But have you ever thought you could do more than just the obvious? You know, get outside the box.

Being extremely organized means you have to be a self-motivator. Being a self-motivator means you can work at home. Are you following me? All those baby steps

God led me to take have given me the ability to complete my task at hand. All the different chapels that I have worked at, combined with all the different people and living overseas, added to all the deployments mixed with all the moves, then combined with my gifts has led me to this moment, sitting on my couch writing these words.

Maybe some people are more like my husband, who knew from seventh grade he wanted to be a doctor. I know for a fact that many are born with the God-given talent and knowledge to complete their dreams.

Then there are people like me who slowly come to the realization, through many trials and life experiences, what their purpose has become. I can honestly say I've never had a dream *per se*, as much as I knew that I had a purpose. I have always been driven by the fact that my existence was not to achieve one certain dream, other than being purposeful.

The two to three-year stint at my new base would allow me enough time to make a difference to someone's life. Whether in my husband's life or in a stranger's life, God would give me an opportunity to make a difference.

I cannot express how cathartic it is to write these words. The devil is so good with his lies and I am so good at thinking less of myself. We are beautifully and won-derfully made. These words alone should motivate us to complete our dreams, but they don't. Whether fear, fear of failure or maybe fear of success, we become so comfortable in our lives that we do not want things to change, because with change will come discomfort of some sort.

I am not a therapist and this discussion should not become a therapy session. What should happen is while you are reading this, quietly ask God what direction your life should be heading. You need to ask God what you should be doing with your talents. All those happy and sad moments in your life can bring support to others. Even if you failed miserably through an experience, it is a great learning tool for others.

My husband and I have shared our almost failed marriage after medical school. We both lost sight of each other and focused on the wrong goal. Now we both have a testimony we can share. Thanks to God, we can bring hope to other couples. Your life is so chalked full of testimonies; you just have to work with God to pull it all together.

"But where do I start?" That is a good question. If your path is not clearly marked for you, then you will have to start praying for opened doors. Make sure the door is not already opened, and you just don't want to go through. We often can ask for guidance and when God answers, we say, "Well, God really didn't mean that."

You can start by volunteering. My girlfriend did this when we were overseas and this led to a civil service job. I know for certain that if you start taking steps of faith,

God will direct you on the correct path. Just be open, because it may get uncomfortable for a while. You may need to stretch and grow, but I promise obeying God and following His path for your life is so fulfilling.

God has plans for you. Are you ready for His future?

1. Sit and think about what natural skills you have.
    Begin to list them. (Note: nothing is too small or
    silly.)

    _____

    _____

    _____

2. When is the last time you prayed about your future?
    If it has been awhile, read Jeremiah 29:11 and begin
    to pray for God's plan.

    _____

    _____

3. What lies is the devil telling you? Now ask God what
    he thinks about those lies. Give the lies and doubts
    to God!

    _____

    _____

    _____

4. What is holding you back from working toward God's plan? List some small things you can do now to prepare for the future. (God's timing is everything.)

_____

_____

_____

POINT TO PONDER

What does "prosper" mean to you? Does your meaning of "prosper" and God's meaning of "prosper" coincide?

TEN

Free Lunch

He who has been stealing must steal no longer, but must work, doing something useful with his own hands, that he may have something to share with those in need.

—EPHESIANS 4:28, NIV

Once, I was reading one of my husband's medical magazines. In the magazine was an article talking about a doctor who'd had enough of frivolous lawsuits so he closed up shop. The proverbial straw for the doctor was a female patient that sued because of a drug that was prescribed. The patient received a notice from lawyers stating that side effects have been linked to this particular drug, so the patient sued because of the potential of harm. She, herself, had not had any harmful side effects. When she was surveyed concerning the doctor, she stated, "He was a good doctor. I am sad to see him leave."

Then the interviewer asked, "If you liked him, why did you sue him?"

Her answer, "Well, I felt I really deserved the money."

As a child and maybe a huge hunk of my young adult life, I have always thought the phrase "no free lunch" meant that there was always an angle, that someone was trying to swindle something out of you. Now I think that the phrase is talking about how someone always has to pay, whether it is you or the other person. I know that those two meanings do overlap.

How many things do we do, according to society's standard, that we consider harmless: monies that we take because we believe that the government will pay or the insurance company will pay, not realizing the good name that we have sullied, taxes we just hiked up, or the insurance rates that we just increased or cancelled?

Don't even try and twist my words here. I am not saying that lawsuits are bad, but how many people can you name that make their livelihood out of potential lawsuits? What they see is free money. However, here are the facts: someone has to pay. There is no free lunch. Here is another fact. If you are stretching any truth to receive money, you are stealing. You can justify it all day. Jump up and down and scream and call me names. But stealing is stealing, and God will hold you accountable.

FEMA was accounting for the money given during one of the major hurricanes. There was a neighborhood that received no damage, but people in the neighborhood placed claims. What was going through these people's minds? I can see one thief among many, but at what point does the many lose sight of reality? Is it because your neighbor is bragging about stealing so you wanted to steal also? Or is it that they bragged about how you can get free money from the government, you just need to tell a little lie?

What makes a whole community go astray? Please spare me the society jargon about being poor. There are lots of poor people, good Christian poor that would be insulted if you insinuated that because they are poor means they would steal. People steal because they want something that they are not willing to work toward.

How many times has a teenager rung you up in a store and given you too much money? Did you give it back or walk off like you hit the lottery?

Once, I was at a one-shop store, and I was purchasing plastic tumblers. They were a dollar apiece. When I put them on the counter, I stacked them together. So when the lady rang them up, she counted them as one item not six. I had to stand over in the customer service line to pay for the other five tumblers. Not fun but very necessary.

No matter how you try and justify a situation, wrong is wrong and stealing is stealing. My choices were simple: either put back the five I did not pay for or pay for the five. And by the way, I did not notice I had not paid until I was almost out the door. I know, check your receipt before you walk.

My point is this—honesty is becoming so scarce.

It should not be an extraordinary act when you return an item that was not yours to begin with. Lawsuits should not be a means to get extra money. Government programs are set up to help the needy not the "I wanty."

I should not have to discuss the basic rules of stealing that are taught in kindergarten, but here we are anyway. Many of you may be thinking, *I have never stolen anything*. Well, let us discuss another version of stealing.

Have you ever belonged to a women's group and when it came time for a potluck there was always one woman who came but did not contribute? Maybe it was not one woman but many? Do the same people in your group work while others just take?

Things are always done, so you just sit back and enjoy. I am not talking about single events; I am talking about constant taking, the thought process of "let them do it."

You often see it in a church when the same dutiful members slave away while others just party and enjoy someone else's labor. The person that thinks they deserve the front of the line service, and if there is a handout, they deserve the freebies—that single-minded person who thinks about the "me" instead of the many, who then becomes the vacuum that will suck the life out of the giver when there is not even a need.

Time is so precious, yet many don't even question when they waste someone else's time. If you, yourself, are not willing to take the time toward a project, then you should be very grateful to the workers who are willing to share their time.

We all have schedules to maintain and no person is more important than the other. If you are arrogant enough to think that your time is more precious than someone else's, then you really need to reevaluate your thoughts. If you have time to socialize, then you have time to give. "Well, I only have enough time to come for an hour." Great, then maybe one week you can take an hour and come early to work and then leave. We are not to be takers in this world. We are put on this earth to glorify God and to be in His service.

I am not telling you that you have to stop socializing. Do not be a brat about this. Stop and evaluate how you can serve God. Do not make the same people do the work. Give. Just give once in awhile. If we all took turns, then the burden would not cause burnout. If you are burning out, then you need to stop and socialize.

Another theft that occurs without notice is stealing someone's credit. How many times have you worked on a project and someone came along and stole the credit for your hard work. There is no good way to say, "Hey, stop lying! I did the work," without looking well, just bitter and dumb, especially when it is a public recognition.

My mother taught me that you are to be a silent worker, especially since you are working for the glory of God not for the glory of yourself. I once worked with two other ladies to perform a combined Catholic and Protestant Christmas musical at our naval chapel. Regrettably, I had asked a layman to do the directing, and he was more interested in the attention than in the mission. I did all the grunt work and even had to fight a few battles to keep the children in the performance, only to have the director take all the credit for things he did not do. Now, let me make this clear. It was the chaplain that made a mistake when he publicly thanked the person for putting the musical together, but it was solely that person's responsibility to say, "I only directed the music. It was so-and-so that did all the work to put the musical together." To me, this is when character is made or broken—when you willingly steal from someone as a thief in the night. Unfortunately, this has not happened to me only once but rather many times.

Every time this happens to me, I am reminded by God what I am working for: Him. "So likewise you, when you have done all those things which you are commanded, say, 'We are unprofitable servants. We have done what was our duty to do'" (Luke 17:10 NKJV). God gives me the strength to continue His work, but stealing the credit from someone may be enough for others just to call it quits. If you're not working for God, you're working for the devil and ten minutes of clapping better make you happy, because you will be held accountable for your actions.

I could write on and on about this subject of stealing, but a time constraint does not allow me the luxury. So, I am going to list a few more thefts and I need you to stop and list your own.

Stealing someone's joy. Something wonderful has happened, but not to you, so you are going to make sure others are not happy either.

Stealing the limelight. Everyone is gathered for another purpose, but you are not getting the attention you think you deserve.

Stealing someone's good name. You are bored and you know some juicy gossip. You know it is most likely not true, but boy is it fun to talk about people.

It is time for you to ask the Holy Spirit to show you what you have purposefully or inadvertently taken from others.

We see stealing as a crime when something tangible is taken. As Christians, we need to look at the stealing of concepts: things that society views as getting ahead in life. These are concepts, which we selfishly take from one another that we view as disposable. That is until it is taken from us.

Jesus never stole ideas or sullied someone's name, even when it meant His life. We are representatives of God. There are no free lunches and you need to think twice before you take from someone, and what price is being paid for what you took.

What example have you set for you peers? People are watching.

1. What is stealing?

_____

_____

_____

2. Many times juries give monetary awards based on emotions and pity. What harm is there in taking the monetary award?

_____

_____

_____

3. Many would say you are not stealing if someone willingly does something for you. Give a biblical argument for or against that statement.

_____

_____

_____

4. Many would say it is your fault for allowing someone to take credit for anything you do. Does this statement stand up biblically?

_____

_____

_____

POINT TO PONDER

In your arguments, was your argument based on your beliefs or God's beliefs? Were you able to remove the "self" from the argument and focus on God? (Resource: Proverbs)

Christian Citizen

*Therefore, get rid of all moral filth and the evil
that is so prevalent and humbly accept the word
planted in you, which can save you. Do not merely
listen to the word, and so deceive yourselves. Do
what it says. Anyone who listens to the word but
does not do what is says is like a man who looks
at his face in a mirror and, after looking at himself, goes away and immediately forgets what he
looks like. But the man who looks intently into
the perfect law that gives freedom, and contin-
ues to do this, not forgetting what he has heard,
but doing it, he will be blessed in what he does.*

—JAMES 1:21–25, NIV

I am not going to talk to you about politics specifically. I
will say that you need to become a good citizen. If you
are a typical military family, you may move every two to
three years; of course, some have homesteaded. But the

moving makes it difficult to become a voter. You may be registered, but when it comes time to vote, you get lazy about your absentee ballet. You might even take a bad attitude, like I unfortunately have, and say that it does not matter anyway, because they don't count the absentee votes.

It *does* matter. You and your husband fight for this country, so along with all the people in the States, your opinion certainly *does* matter. As Christians, you need to vote and make a difference instead of whining about how special interest groups are ruining this country.

Stop listening to the media or Hollywood and believing that your Christian beliefs make you a bigot or a hate-monger. It is amazing to me that society has bought into believing that Muslims are peaceful when their Koran teaches them to kill the unbelievers and Christians are warring hate-mongers, and the Bible teaches us to love our enemies.

Be proud of your Christian heritage. You need to remember that the Bible says: "But he who denies Me before men will be denied before the angels of God" (Luke 12:9, NKJV). Read your Bible and get to know exactly what God says about issues. This is mandatory to becoming a good citizen. You need to stop being lazy about feeding yourself with the word. A few years ago, I found myself just reading Christian self-help books and listening to televised sermons. While these are good, you are relying on others to feed you and are dependent on their interpretation of the Bible. It is imperative that you spend time with God alone and read his word. This allows God to talk with you and build a personal relationship.

Being an election year, the news is talking about voters. It used to be that Christian voters would vote according to their beliefs. Well, that has now changed. Christian voters vote according to their economical needs. Wow. Why are we labeling ourselves "Christian"? If we no longer have our beliefs as the driving force, meaning God first, then what is in the name? If our wants are our driving force, then we are just like every other voter in society. How can we get upset with what is going on in our society if we are not willing to take a stand for God?

To become a good citizen, you need to educate yourself with the issues that are being pushed through by our politicians. These days, information is very easy to come by. Be careful though, and do not get caught up in someone else's opinion.

Sorry to say, the news is no longer just the facts about a particular story. The reporter often places a spin by certain carefully chosen words used to inflame a response. Sadly, most people do not hear or understand the concept. Therefore, they walk around with an opinion on a subject that was not their original thought. They hear hot button, politically correct rhetoric, then the fear of society thinking they are a bigot or hateful, sways the listener to the side of society. This is where your knowledge of God's word is very important.

If you know what God has instructed on a subject, then your path should be clear.

Do not buy into the name-calling that the liberals have labeled Christians. Our faith hates the sin, not the sinner. Liberals want you to believe that the two are the same. "If you hate my lifestyle, then you are a bigot."

More and more we are hearing blatant blaspheming of God and his Son. If it were any other faith, there would be talk of hate speech. Since it is concerning Christianity, you hear more and more that it is freedom of speech. Just recently a comedian, during her acceptance speech of an award, cursed Jesus. There was a small outcry, but what struck me was how small the outcry was.

If Allah were spoken about in that manner, I guarantee you would have people asking for a boycott of her concerts. Talk of hate toward such a peace-loving people like the Muslims would not be tolerated. All the Christians got was the excuse that she is a comedian who always pushes the envelope.

My question is, why do comedians get to hide under the umbrella of "it was just a joke" when really it was their hateful opinion spun in disgusting humor? Since when did hate become funny? The number one reason we are seeing interest groups gain legal ground is because they are willing to put their money and time into their beliefs. Christians, well, we have become so complacent that we cannot be bothered with politics. We are so concerned with soccer, cheerleading and what college the kids will attend that we have not even noticed our rights have passed being stomped on; they are gone.

Christians have not lost the fight; they never got in the fight. Christians are so busy being busy that the center of our Christian world, which is God, is pushed aside. Oh, we go to church, sing and tithe, but we forget that God belongs in all aspects of our lives, and not just on Sundays.

We are representatives of God and we need to ask Him for guidance during our elections. Our votes should reflect our Christian beliefs. As Christians, we need to remember that we are setting an example for our children. It is important that they understand there is always time for the important things in life. God is our main focus. If our lives are too busy, then we need to start trimming up the fat. Being a good citizen is not fat. If you do not take the time now and vote according to your Christian beliefs, then in a few years you may be sadly surprised when Christianity becomes illegal.

Can you pray in school? Can your child mention God in

a speech? Can a Christian organization be sued for having God in their bylaws? Have the Ten Commandments been banned from courtrooms?

I can go on and on. Christian rights are flying out the door, and we just keep on going like it is normal. So, don't kid yourself. In ten years it may just be completely illegal to be a Christian. It is *your* responsibility to vote. Do it while you still have the right.

1. Do you know what separation of church and state actually means? Do you know where to find the information?

_____

_____

_____

2. What is a hate speech? What does freedom of speech entail?

_____

_____

_____

3. How important are the Ten Commandments? Do you feel they are outdated? Is your answer based on "self" or on God?

_____

_____

4. Are you a voter? Do you know how to vote or register?

_____

_____

_____

POINT TO PONDER

Do you ever find yourself mumbling at the news, disgusted by politics? Why don't you do something about it? Why have Christians become so complacent? Have you ever thought the devil has beaten us by allowing us to get completely satisfied in our big houses with our many toys? What are a few rights anyway?

TWELVE

"Who is My Neighbor?"

LUKE 10:26–37

When you read the parable of the Good Samaritan, you may think to yourself, "Yes, I would help my neighbor." But who is your neighbor?

As Christians, we tend to either consciously or unconsciously isolate ourselves. I am not even going to say we isolate ourselves from the world. We can isolate ourselves from social classes or someone we deem to be beneath us.

You quickly look over the newcomer and assess whether or not they seem worthy of your greeting. If they are dressed fairly appropriate according to your standards, then you make your gracious move. Does this statement seem harsh? Am I far off base? So, if a 400-pound woman came in with untidy clothes and dirty hair, you would be the first to bust a gut to greet her?

Face it—most of us would fall under the category of the priest and the Levite. As women, we tend to judge and categorize each person we meet. Being married to a Navy man for twenty years, I have seen this malicious act many times, and sometimes toward me. How can we claim to be Christian women and act so coldly toward each other?

See, your arrogance does not just affect you; you are a representative of God. You may not understand why desiring to stick with "your kind" is a problem, but God did not put you in this world to isolate yourself.

His last statement is clear: "Go and do likewise." You are to "love your neighbor as yourself". Self-importance has always been a mind-boggler to me. When I see this behavior of "I am superior to you," I am reminded of Deuteronomy 6:16, NKJV, which states, "Thou shalt not tempt the Lord thy God..." I find it very arrogant that some women tend to take credit for their appearance and use it as a weapon toward simple-looking women. Each human's features were selected by God for His glory. Do you really think God is going to allow you to abuse one of His creations without consequences?

Now you are wondering how judging people makes you a priest or a Levite. Well, both of these people passed on the other side of the road just because they did not want to get involved with the half-dead naked stranger. They made a judgment call just like most of us do.

We look at people and if they look like they have their lives together, we deem it okay to get involved with them. How fair is that? Have your ever thought about the fact that God brings people into our lives for a reason, even if for a brief moment or a brief smile to say, "Hey, welcome"?

I have mentioned before that we have the power in us to make or break a stranger's day. Just smiling or saying hello to someone is more powerful than people understand. That gesture can make a stranger feel worthwhile.

I love to tell the story about the man at the tube stop in West Ruislip, England. My husband and I lived in London, and every day that we got on the tube (underground), my husband would stop and speak to the gentlemen selling the tickets. On the first, "How are you today," the gentleman looked at my husband like my husband was on drugs. But each time we would go by, my husband would greet the gentlemen with a statement. It took what seemed like months, but then one day my husband and I were in conversation with each other when the ticket salesman spoke to us. We were both so stunned that my husband barely stammered out a, "Fine, thank you."

See, most people just treated the salesman as a machine, looking past him. Soon the salesman acted like a machine with no self-worth. "How on earth can I apply the Good Samaritan parable to my military life?" Well, let us try and do that.

You are standing in a room of properly powdered, scented and stylishly dressed woman. Each woman is carefully posed with their $300 purse on her shoulder or on her arm. You notice that several women keep glancing over to a certain direction and making faces. You cannot see what they are seeing, but you can tell by their expressions, they are not pleased. As you walk in that direction, you see a well-tattooed female in wrinkled clothes sitting by herself and looking very out of place. She is wearing an expression of "get me out of here." See, the priest and Levites have already made their stance by ignoring her. What will you do?

I have been there. Oh, I do not have any tattoos, and I never wear wrinkled clothes, but I have still been there. I was probably not in the up-to-date styles; maybe I was having a bad hair day. Who knows what it takes for a group of females to act like sharks? We have all seen that out-of-place female that could use a friendly face. What will it cost you to be kind?

God may have blessed your husband with rank, so do not abuse that position. There is no rank in the Christian family. Ladies, you have no right to make lower-ranking wives feel less than adequate or make them jump through hoops to make you feel superior.

Make up your mind now that you are going to be a Good Samaritan. It costs you nothing to show some teeth and extend your hand. As military spouses, we have forfeited greatly. Some have given up great jobs or careers. We all have left family and shed tears.

Let us find a common ground in God and learn to love each other.

1. Do you find yourself an isolationist? Do you know
    what one is? How open are you to speaking with
    someone socially that you deem beneath you or not
    in your league? Does this behavior seem normal to
    you? What does the Bible say about this behavior?
    Base your argument for or against?

    _____

    _____

    _____

2. What is arrogance? (Get the dictionary ladies.)
    Describe it. Do you fit any of the descriptions?

    _____

    _____

    _____

POINT TO PONDER

When someone has placed extreme judgment on you, do you remember how you felt? Looking at the other person's viewpoint, were they justified in judging you? Have you ever stood in judgment of someone else for the same act you were accused? Then why, when we remember all that pain, would we willingly subject someone else to the same pain? Have you ever thought that God was trying to teach you empathy or maybe God was trying to teach you to stop judging?

THIRTEEN

Finale Stretch

The Lord is good, a refuge in times of trouble.
He cares for those who trust in him...

—Nahum 1:7, NIV

You have a date. He is coming home. You never knew time could stretch to such a slow crawl. In your mind, you have fantasized exactly what the homecoming is going to be like.

Of course, you have thought about this so much that do you really think anything could hold up to your fantasy? Are you setting yourself up for failure? We tend to do this to ourselves. A big event is coming, and we role-play in our minds. We have the perfect body, and we're wearing the perfect outfit. Everything that comes out of our mouth is mesmerizing. We are the perfect person. Then reality hits.

You cannot find a perfect outfit on the market, because everything was made for a hanger. Anything of a realistic cut has some bizarre pattern or flower. Humidity is high, so your hair is either a lion's mane or as flat and slick as a slip-and-slide. And yes, the stress bump arrives along with your period. This is reality. It is not pretty but really funny if you let it be. Once you start setting the bar too high, everyone gets disappointed.

When my husband was coming back from Iraq, I had 17 years of marriage to fall back on. The house was clean, but I did not kill myself. You are worthless if you exhausted yourself with last-minute cleaning and cooking. Food was in the fridge and desserts on standby. I left his options open. If he wanted something cooked, we could do it together, or we could go out to eat. There was nothing for me to get my feelings hurt over. I left lots of options open.

Why do we do things the way we want them and then get mad when he does not desire the same thing? The answer is, because during the deployment you had the final say. Now, he is back and wants to resume where the two of you left off. He did not experience the last few months with all your trials with the kids or mechanical issues. He does not know about the everyday issues that happened in your life. As far as he is concerned, home life stood still.

The best thing you could do for homecoming is prepare. Do not make fun of the homecoming classes that the military offers. They have been doing homecomings for many years. They will give you so much information. You know what? I was impressed by these classes; the instructors were spouses like us, many with multiple tours and experiences to share.

Personally, I enjoy listening to a speaker who has been in my shoes. You can have all the degrees in the world, but I am impressed with the spouse who has mileage. They are the ones like me that will tell you what works and what does not work.

When you start preparing for the homecoming, have your study group start praying for your reunion. With your preparation, get the major spring-cleaning you want to do completed a few weeks before the arrival date. Do not take on any new jobs. If you have not painted the upstairs by now, two weeks before homecoming is not a good time to take on the task. Dates change and yes, sometimes they can move forward.

For security reasons, keep the arrival dates secure. If extended family does not understand, then too bad. You really should have only immediate family for a few weeks anyway. They will cover the details why in your reunion brief. Let your husband acclimate.

Send extended family members the pamphlets that the military has on reunions. This is about your spouse. Use the resources the military has set up for extended family. The military can explain the process of reuniting families. Then let it go. There is no reason to start a family war weeks before your spouse comes home.

I could write mountains of things not to do concerning homecoming, but the best thing I think I could say to you is keep it simple. If you want a party with a big bang, then wait until he comes home and include him in the planning. Include him in everything; this is key to your marriage. Give your pride to God and let your husband slowly take charge again. Be careful here. Do not dump everything on him at once. This should be a slow process; do not exclude him. You are a family.

Your spouse may want to change everything you have set up in the last few months. Will this hurt your feelings? His method of paying the bills may not be as organized as yours, but that does not mean it is wrong. Your spouse may want to spend money that you have saved during deployment. Keep the communication going; discuss things. He may also want an explanation of what you spent during the deployment. Have you thought about what it is going to be like when you give over the checkbook? How will you handle this much change again? Transition can be rough. The tendency is to exclude your spouse when he begins to exert himself back into the home.

Pray, pray, pray. This is so important. It is so easy to lose your temper and snap during the transition time. It is important to ask God to guide your actions and your mouth. Invite God into every aspect of your marriage, including your bedroom. Don't get queasy on me. Sex was made for marriage, but you two have been apart for months. The movies are a great big lie. If you are expecting a great love scene, well you may get it, or you may get very disappointed. Ask God to give you great passion for your husband. Make sure to ask him to take away any insecurities you may feel about yourself.

It is so funny. I am in my forties and have more bumps and dimples than I care to admit, but my husband still finds me sexy. Thank you, God.

Women...well, we see every imperfection on our bodies. Men, thank God, see with different eyes. I do not understand it, but I am very grateful.

Once again, pray and keep it simple. Your marriage is important to God. He wants your family to stay whole. Go to God before any trouble starts.

POINT TO PONDER

You have been in control for the last few months. Your spouse may want to change many things around from the way you did it. Will this hurt your feelings? Does this mean your way is wrong? How will you handle this much change again? What are your resources? What did you do to prepare yourself for these events? Did you include God? How is your prayer life? Do you understand that God wants to protect you from distress and is one thought away?

Corresponding Verses for Study

NEW INTERNATIONAL VERSION

ACCOUNT

HEBREWS 4:13: Nothing in all creation is hidden from God's sight. Everything is uncovered and laid bare before the eyes of him to whom we must give account.

PSALMS 7:15–16: He who digs a hole and scoops it out falls into the pit he has made. The trouble he causes recoils on himself; his violence comes down on his own head.

ADULTERY

PROVERBS 6:32: But a man who commits adultery lacks judgment; whoever does so destroys himself.

ATTITUDE

PHILIPPIANS 2:5: Your attitude should be the same as that of Christ Jesus.

EPHESIANS 4:22–24: You were taught, with regard to your former way of life, to put off your old self, which is being corrupted by its deceitful desires; to be made new in the attitude of your minds; and to put on the new self, created to be like God in true righteousness and holiness.

BELIEF

JAMES 2:19: You believe that there is one God. Good! Even the demons believe that-and shudder.

CALLING

HEBREWS 5:4: No one takes this honor upon himself; he must be called by God, just as Aaron was.

HEBREWS 6:10: God is not unjust; he will not forget your work and the love you have shown him as you have helped his people and continue to help them.

CONDUCT

ACTS 2:46–47, NKJV: So continuing daily with one accord in the temple, and breaking bread from house to house, they ate their food with gladness and simplicity of heart, praising God and having favor with all people. And the Lord added to the church daily those who were being saved.

I Peter 3:8–9: Finally, all of you, live in harmony with one another; be sympathetic, love as brothers, be compassionate and humble. Do not repay evil with evil or insult with insult, but with blessing, because to this you were called so that you may inherit a blessing.

Ephesians 5:15–20: Be very careful, then, how you live-not as unwise but as wise, making the most of every opportunity, because the days are evil. Therefore do not be foolish, but understand what the Lord's will is. Do not get drunk on wine, which leads to debauchery. Instead, be filled with the Spirit. Speak to one another with psalms, hymns and spiritual songs. Sing and make music in your heart to the Lord, always giving thanks to God the Father for everything, in the name of our Lord Jesus Christ.

Philippians 3:12–14: Not that I have already obtained all this, or have already been made perfect, but I press on to take hold of that for which Christ Jesus took hold of me. Brothers, I do not consider myself yet to have taken hold of it. But one thing I do: Forgetting what is behind and straining toward what is ahead, I press on toward the goal to win the prize for which God has called me heavenward in Christ Jesus.

I PETER 2:1–2: Therefore, rid yourselves of all malice and all deceit, hypocrisy, envy, and slander of every kind. Like newborn babies, crave pure spiritual milk, so that by it you may grow up in your salvation, now that you have tasted that the Lord is good.

I PETER 4:3: For you have spent enough time in the past doing what pagans choose to do- living in debauchery, lust, drunkenness, orgies, carousing and detestable idolatry.

HEBREWS 13:16: And do not forget to do good and to share with others, for with such sacrifices God is pleased.

PROVERBS 1:7: The fear of the Lord is the beginning of knowledge, but fools despise wisdom and discipline.

PHILIPPIANS 2:14–16: Do everything without complaining or arguing, so that you may become blameless and pure, children of God without fault in a crooked and depraved generation, in which you shine like stars in the universe as you hold out the word of life- in order that I may boast on the day of Christ that I did not run or labor for nothing.

DECEIVING GOD

GALATIANS 6:7–8: Do not be deceived: God cannot be mocked. A man reaps what he sows. The one who sows to please his sinful nature, from that nature will reap destruction; the one who sows to please the Spirit, from the Spirit will reap eternal life.

DISCERNMENT

PHILIPPIANS 1:9–11: And this is my prayer: that your love may abound more and more in knowledge and depth of insight, so that you may be able to discern what is best and may be pure and blameless until the day of Christ, filled with the fruit of righteousness that comes through Jesus Christ- to the glory and praise of God.

DISCIPLINE

HEBREWS 12:11: No discipline seems pleasant at the time, but painful. Later on, however, it produces a harvest of righteousness and peace for those who have been trained by it.

DRUNK

EPHESIANS 5:15–18: Be very careful, then, how you live—not as unwise but as wise, making the most of every opportunity, because the days are evil. Therefore do not be foolish, but understand what the Lord's will is. Do not get drunk on wine, which leads to debauchery. Instead, be filled with the Spirit.

ESCAPE CORRUPTION

2 PETER 1:3–4: His divine power has given us everything we need for life and godliness through our knowledge of him who called us by his own glory and goodness. Through these he has given us his very great and precious promises, so that through them you may participate in the divine nature and escape the corruption in the world cased by evil desires.

ENCOURAGEMENT

PSALMS 18:28–29: You, O Lord, keep my lamp burning; my God turns my darkness into light. With your help I can advance against a troop; with my God I can scale a wall.

HEBREWS 12:2–3: Let us fix our eyes on Jesus, the aut hor and perfecter of our faith, who for the joy set before him endured the cross, scorning its shame, and sat down at the right hand of the throne of God. Consider him who endured such opposition from sinful men, so that you will not grow weary and lose heart.

2 PETER 1:5–8: For this very reason, make every effort to add to your faith goodness; and to goodness, knowledge;

and to knowledge, self-control; and to self-control, perseverance; and to perseverance, godliness; and to godliness, brotherly kindness; and to brotherly kindness, love. For if you possess these qualities in increasing measure, they will keep you from being ineffective and unproductive in you knowledge of our Lord Jesus Christ.

ENVY/WISDOM

JAMES 3:13–16, NKJV: Who is wise and understanding among you? Let him show by good conduct *that* his works *are done* in the meekness of wisdom. But if you have bitter envy and self-seeking in your hearts, do not boast and lie against the truth. This wisdom does not descend from above, but *is* earthly, sensual, demonic. For where envy and self-seeking *exist*, confusion and every evil thing *are* there.

FAITH

HEBREWS 11:6: And without faith it is impossible to please God, because anyone who comes to him must believe that he exists and that he rewards those who earnestly seek him.

FALSE RELIGION/TRADITIONS

COLOSSIANS 2:8: See to it that no one takes you captive through hollow and deceptive philosophy, which depends on human tradition and the basic principles of this world rather than on Christ.

GIFTS OF GOD/SERVICE

I PETER 4:9–11: Offer hospitality to one another without grumbling. Each one should use whatever gift he has received to serve others, faithfully administering God's grace in its various forms. If anyone speaks, he should do it as one speaking the very words of God. If anyone serves, he should do it with the strength God provides, so that in all things God may be praised through Jesus Christ. To him be the glory and the power for ever and ever. Amen.

GOVERNMENT

TITUS 3:1–2: Remind the people to be subject to rulers and authorities, to be obedient, to be ready to do whatever is good, to slander no one, to be peaceable and considerate, and to show true humility toward all men.

LUKE 20:25: "Then give to Caesar what is Caesar's, and to God what is God's."

GRACE

ISAIAH 30:18: Yet the Lord longs to be gracious to you; he rises to show you compassion. For the Lord is a God of justice. Blessed are all who wait for him!

PSALMS 25:16–18: Turn to me and be gracious to me, for I am lonely and afflicted. The troubles of my heart have multiplied; free me from my anguish. Look upon my affliction and my distress and take away all my sins.

GRIEVING THE HOLY SPIRIT

EPHESIANS **4:29–32**: Do not let any unwholesome talk come out of your mouths, but only what is helpful for building others up accordin g to their needs, that it may benefit those who listen. And do not grieve the Holy Spirit of God, with whom you were sealed for the day of redemption. Get rid of all bitterness, rage and anger, brawling and slander, along with every form of malice. Be kind and compassionate to one another, forgiving each other, just as in Christ God forgave you.

HOLY

HEBREWS **10:10**: And by that will, we have been made holy through the sacrifice of the body of Jesus Christ once for all.

JUSTICE

LEVITICUS **19:15**: Do not pervert justice; do not show partiality to the poor or favoritism to the great, but judge your neighbor fairly.

LIFE WITH CHRIST

COLOSSIANS **2:6:** So then, just as you received Christ Jesus as Lord, continue to live in him, rooted and built up in him, strengthened in the faith as you were taught, and over-flowing with thankfulness.

LOVE

I PETER **4:8:** Above all, love each other deeply, because love covers over a multitude of sins.

MOUTH

I PETER **2:23:** When they hurled their insults at him, he did not retaliate; when he suffered, he made no threats.

JAMES **3:9–1:** With the tongue we praise our Lord and Father, and with it we curse men, who have been made in God's likeness. Out of the same mouth come praise and cursing. My brothers, this should not be. Can both fresh water and salt water flow from the same spring?

JAMES **3:2–6.**

JAMES **1:26,** NKJV: If anyone among you thinks he is religious, and does not bridle his tongue but deceives his own heart, this one's religion *is* useless.

NEAR GOD/SUBMISSION

JAMES **4:7–8**: Submit yourselves, then, to God. Resist the devil, and he will flee from you. Come near to God and he will come near to you…

PERSEVERANCE

JAMES **5:11**: As you know, we consider blessed those who have persevered. You have heard of Job's perseverance and have seen what the Lord finally brought about. The Lord is full of compassion and mercy.

PRAYER

I PETER **5:6–7**: Humble yourselves, therefore, under God's mighty hand, that he may lift you up in due time. Cast all your anxiety on him because he cares for you.

PRAYER/COVET

JAMES **4:2–3**: You want something but don't get it. You kill and covet, but you cannot have what you want. You quarrel and fight. You do not have, because you do not ask God. When you ask, you do not receive, because you ask with wrong motives, that you may spend what you get on your pleasures.

PROPHECY

2 PETER 1:21: For prophecy never had its origin in the will of man, but men spoke from God as they were carried along by the Holy Spirit.

PROSPER

EPHESIANS 1:18: I pray also that the eyes of your heart may be enlightened in order that you may know the hope to which he has called you, the riches of his glorious inheritance in the saints.

PROVERBIAL WOMAN

PROVERBS 31:10–31.

REFUGE

PSALMS 5:11–12: But let all who take refuge in you be glad; let them ever sing for joy. Spread your protection over them, that those who love your name may rejoice in you. For surely, O Lord, you bless the righteous; you surround them with your favor as with a shield.

RESTORING THE SOUL

PSALMS 23.

SALVATION

EPHESIANS 2:8–9: For it is by grace you have been saved, through faith—and this not from yourselves, it is the gift of God—not by works, so that no one can boast.

SELF CONTROL

I PETER 5:8–9: Be self-controlled and alert. Your enemy the devil prowls around like a roaring lion looking for someone to devour. Resist him, standing firm in the faith, because you know that your brothers throughout the world are undergoing the same kind of sufferings.

SELFISH

PHILIPPIANS 2:3–4: Do nothing out of selfish ambition or vain conceit, but in humility consider others better than yourselves. Each of you should look not only to your own interests, but also to the interests of others.

SEXUAL IMMORALITY

EPHESIANS 5:3–7: But among you there must not be even a hint of sexual immorality, or any kind of impurity, or of greed, because these are improper for God's holy people. Nor should there be obscenity, foolish talk or coarse joking, which are out of place, but rather thanksgiving. For this you can be sure: No immoral, impure or greedy person—such a man is an idolater—has any inheritance in the kingdom of Christ and of God. Let no one deceive you with empty words, for because of such things God's wrath comes on those who are disobedient. Therefore do not be partners with them.

1 CORINTHIANS 6:18–20: Flee from sexual immorality. All other sins a man commits are outside his body, but he who sins sexually sins against his own body. Do you not know that your body is a temple of the Holy Spirit, who is in you, whom you have received from God? You are not your own; you were bought at a price. Therefore honor God with your body.

SIN

JAMES 4:17: Anyone, then, who knows the good he ought to do and doesn't do it, sins.

HEBREWS 3:12–13: See to it, brothers, that none of you has a sinful, unbelieving heart that turns away from the living God. But encourage one another daily, as long as it is called Today, so that none of you may be hardened by sin's deceitfulness.

ISAIAH 30:1: Woe to the obstinate children, declares the Lord, to those who carry out plans that are not mine, forming an alliance, but not by my Spirit, heaping sin upon sin.

STRENGTH

I PETER 5:10: And the God of all grace, who called you to his eternal glory in Christ, after you have suffered a little while, will himself restore you and make you strong, firm and steadfast.

SUBMISSION/ATTITUDE

EPHESIANS 5:21: Submit to one another out of reverence for Christ.

TEACHER

JAMES 3:1: Not many of you should presume to be teachers, my brothers, because you know that we who teach will be judged more strictly.

TEMPTATION

HEBREWS 2:18: Because he himself suffered when he was tempted, he is able to help those who are being tempted.

I PETER 1:8–9: Though you have not seen him, you love him; and even though you do not see him now, you believe in him and are filled with an inexpressible and glorious joy, for you are receiving the goal of your faith, the salvation of your souls.

HEBREWS 4:15–16: For we do not have a high priest who is unable to sympathize with our weaknesses, but we have one who has been tempted in every way, just as we are-yet was without sin. Let us then approach the throne of grace with confidence, so that we may receive mercy and find grace to help us in our time of need.

TRUST

PROVERBS **3:5–6**: Trust in the Lord with all your heart and lean not on your own understanding; in all your ways acknowledge him, and he will make your paths straight.

WAIT ON THE LORD

PSALMS **27**.